50 ANY-SIZE TRAVEL QUILT BLOCKS
BIG CITY BLOCKS

by Rita Weiss & Linda Causee

Before You Start

Choose the block you want to make. Inside this book, you will find a self-loading CD that contains 50 Big City Blocks foundation patterns in four sizes. The files on the CD are easily opened using Adobe® Reader®. If you don't have Adobe® Reader® on your computer you can get a free download at http://www.adobe.com/. The site provides easy, step-by-step instructions for the download.

When you are ready to make your quilt, simply print out the required pattern(s) for your block(s) in the size you desire: 5", 6", 7" or 8". Additional sizes are possible by reducing or enlarging your printer output. If you would like to make a 10" block, you will need to visit your local copy store and enlarge a 5" block by 200% then print it out on 11" x 17" paper.

LEISURE ARTS, INC.
Maumelle, Arkansas

Produced by

Production Team

Creative Directors: Jean Leinhauser
and Rita Weiss

Block Diagrams: April McArthur

Book Design: Linda Causee

Technical Editor: Ann Harnden

Published by Leisure Arts

© 2014 by Leisure Arts, Inc.
104 Champs Blvd., STE 100
Maumelle, AR 72113-6738
www.leisurearts.com

We have made every effort to ensure that these instructions are accurate and complete. We cannot, however, be responsible for human error, typographical mistakes, or variations in individual work.

Library of Congress Control Number: 2014940360

ISBN-13: 978-1-4647-1593-8

Introduction

Who doesn't have a desire to visit famous sites around the world?

Who hasn't wanted to actually see the world's tallest building, a building that leans, or one that looks like a giant basket? Have you wanted to set your sights on a house built on top of a waterfall, or one that looks like a beehive? Have you wanted to view the home of the presidents, or the palace where the English royal family greets crowds on important occasions?

Now what if in addition to visiting all these famous buildings, you could make a fantastic memento of your trip to cover your bed or to hang on a wall?

We may not be able to help you plan your trip, but we can help you with that memento. In this book we've given you a collection of famous buildings that can be recreated with foundation-pieced quilt blocks accented with appliqué and simple embroidery.

Look through the book and make your choice; choose a block which depicts one of your favorites, or choose a block which represents a site you have only dreamed of seeing. You can create an entire quilt by repeating one block, or elect to make a sampler quilt or wall hanging with many different blocks, like the quilts we show on pages 54 to 63.

If you are an experienced quilter, or just a beginner, you may agree that one of the most difficult parts of a project is finding the needed patterns in the necessary sizes. Find the answer to that problem in this book and its enclosed CD! Just place the CD into your computer, click on the block of your choice in the size that you need and print out the patterns you'll need.

If you've forgotten—or if you've never learned how to make a quilt, we've included some basic instructions on the CD as well.

So get ready to add a colorful addition to your home. Make a miniature quilt, a wall hanging, or even a full-size bed quilt, and then be prepared to receive applause from all who visit your home and to enjoy that architectural masterpiece even if you have never seen it in person.

Contents

St. Paul's Cathedral
London, United Kingdom

For more than 1,400 years, a cathedral dedicated to St. Paul has stood at this site, Ludgate Hill, the highest point in the city of London. The present cathedral was designed by England's most famous architect, Sir Christopher Wren and was built between 1675 and 1710.

Note: *Embroider cross at top of dome. Appliqué circular windows after block is completed.*

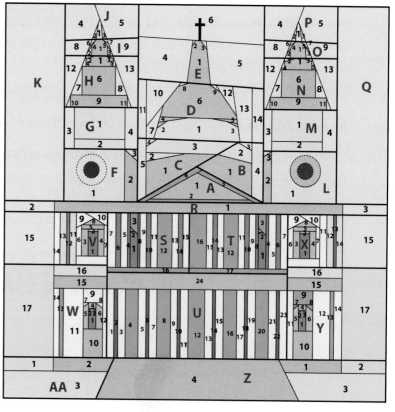

The White House
Washington, DC, USA

The White House at 1600 Pennsylvania Avenue in Washington, DC is the official residence and office of the President of the United States. James Hoban, an Irish-born architect, was the winner of a competition to design the House to be built on a site selected by George Washington. It took eight years to construct the House, which was first occupied by President John Adams in 1800.

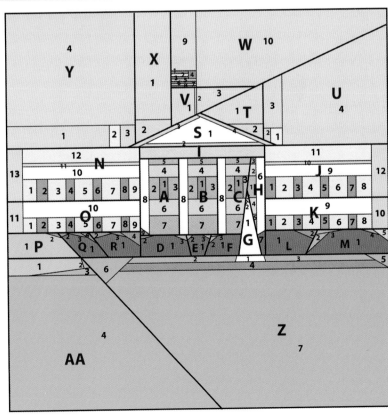

Leaning Tower of Pisa
Pisa, Italy

The "Torre di Pisa" is actually a freestanding bell tower of the cathedral of the city of Pisa. It is, however, known around the world for an unintended tilt to one side. The tilt began during construction from 1173 to 1372 because the ground on which the foundation stands is too soft to support the weight of the tower. The tilt gradually increased for hundreds of years until the tower was stabilized and the tilt partially corrected in 2008 when engineers declared that the Tower had been stabilized and finally stopped moving.

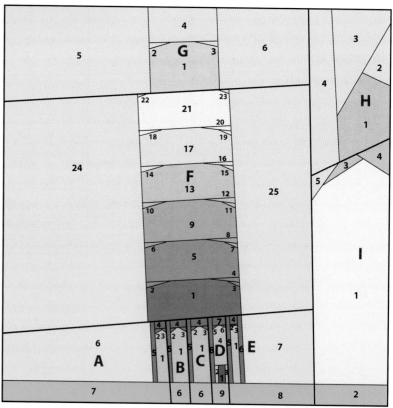

St. Basil's Cathedral

Moscow, Russia

Although it is commonly called St. Basil's, this building is officially "The Cathedral of the Intercession of the Virgin by the Moat." It was built from 1555 to 1561 on orders from the tsar, Ivan the Terrible, and originally contained eight side churches arranged around a ninth church. A tenth church was built in 1588 over the grave of a local saint, Vasily (Basil). The building is still partly in use today as a museum.

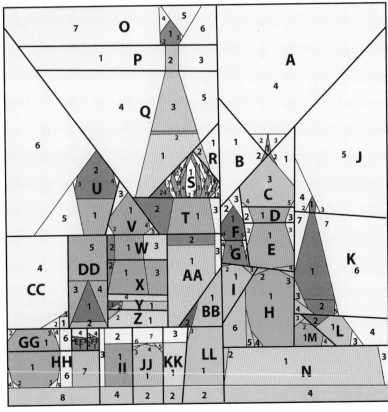

Empire State Building

New York, New York, USA

The Empire State Building is a 103-story building located in midtown Manhattan at the corner of Fifth Avenue and West 34th Street. For nearly 40 years from its completion in 1930, it was the world's tallest building until the World Trade Center was completed. It has a roof height of 1,250 feet, and with its antenna spire included, it stands a total of 1,454 feet high.

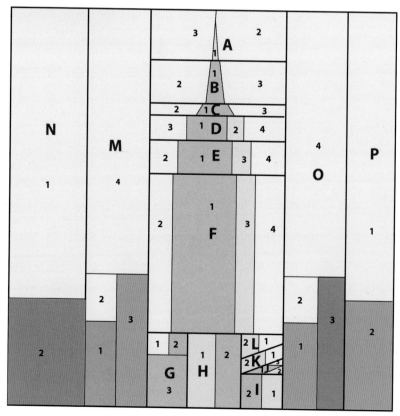

Colosseum
Rome, Italy

The Colosseum is an elliptical amphitheater in the very center of the city of Rome. The Colosseum's original Latin name was Amphitheatrum Flavium, often known in English as the Flavian Amphitheater. It was constructed by emperors of the Flavian dynasty following the reign of the emperor Nero around 70 AD. The theater was rumored to seat over 80,000 people, although modern estimates give that figure as closer to 50,000.

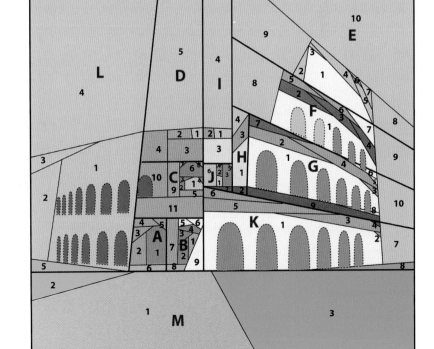

Note: *Appliqué arched openings after block is completed.*

Taj Mahal
Agra, Uttar Pradesh, India

The Taj Mahal, a white marble mausoleum, was built by the Mughal emperor, Shah Jahan, in memory of his third wife, Mumtaz Mahal. The construction, begun around 1632, and completed around 1653, employed thousands of artisans and craftsmen. It is today regarded as the finest example of Mughal architecture, which combines Islamic, Persian, Ottoman, Turkish and Indian architecture.

Note: *Embroider decorative symbol at top of dome.*

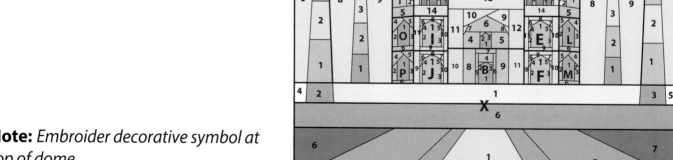

Sydney Opera House
Sydney, Australia

The Sydney Opera House, a multi-performing arts center, opened in Sydney, Australia in 1973. Despite its name, it is used for many different performance types including those of the four key resident companies: Opera Australia, The Australian Ballet, the Sydney Theatre Company, and the Sydney Symphony Orchestra. The facility was designed by the Danish architect , Jørn Utzon. When Utzon received the Pritzer Architecture prize in 2003, the citation read: "There is no doubt that the Sydney Opera House is his masterpiece. It is one of the great iconic buildings of the 20th century, an image of great beauty that has become known throughout the world – a symbol for not only a city, but a whole country and continent."

Space Needle
Seattle, Washington, USA

The Space Needle was built in the Seattle Center for the 1962 World's Fair in Seattle as an observation tower. When it was built at approximately 605 feet, it was the tallest structure west of the Mississippi River. From the top of the Needle, there is a view of the Olympic and Cascade Mountains as well as Mount Rainier, Mount Baker, Elliott Bay, and surrounding islands. It was built to withstand winds of up to 200 miles per hour as well as earthquakes of up to 9.1 magnitudes. In 1999, the city's Landmarks Preservation Board designated it an historic landmark.

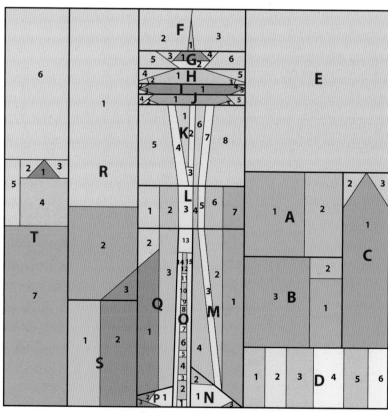

Hotel Del Coronado

Coronado, California, USA

The Hotel Del Coronado is one of the last examples of the wooden Victorian beach resort. Located just across San Diego Bay from the city of San Diego, The Del (as it is sometimes known) is a luxury beachfront hotel. In 1977 the hotel was designated as a national historic landmark and is also a designated California Historical Landmark.

When it opened in 1888, it was known as the largest resort hotel in the world, and over the years it has hosted royalty, presidents, actors and celebrities.

Note: *Appliqué or embroider windows after completing block.*

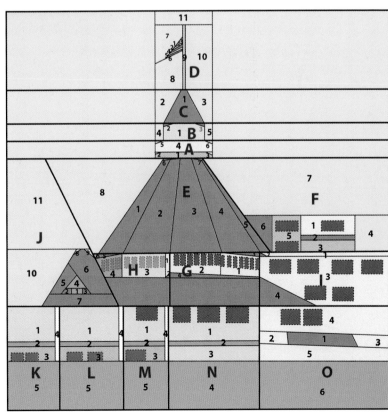

Sears (Willis) Tower
Chicago, Illinois, USA

Named the Sears Tower throughout its history, in 2009 the Willis Group obtained the right to rename the building, as part of their lease. On July 16, 2009, the building was officially renamed Willis Tower. When the building was completed in 1973, it was the tallest building in the United States, even surpassing the World Trade Center in New York.

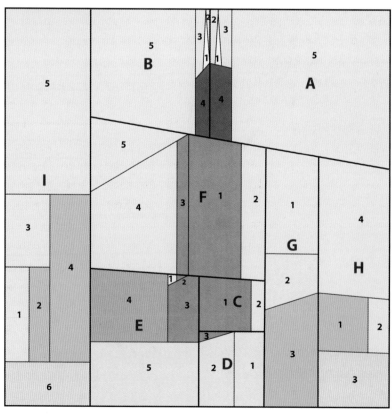

Notre-Dame Cathedral

Paris, France

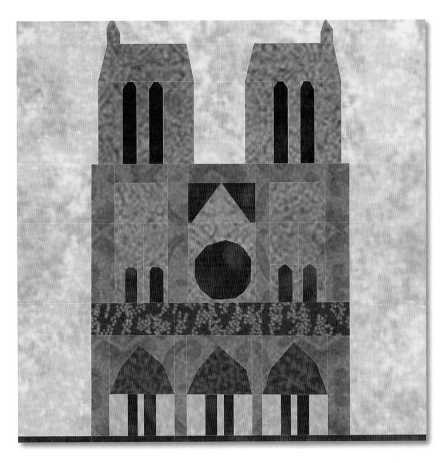

The Notre-Dame Cathedral Paris or Notre-Dame de Paris ("Our Lady of Paris") or simply Notre-Dame is a Catholic Cathedral in Paris, France. Considered one of the finest examples of French Gothic architecture, it is probably the most well known church building in the world. It was among the first buildings in the world to use the arched exterior supports called the "flying buttress." After construction began, stress fractures began to occur. To remedy this, the architects built supports around the outside walls, and many small statues were placed around the outside to serve as supports and water spouts. The famous gargoyles around the outside were actually designed for water run-off. The cathedral was essentially completed by 1345.

Stonehenge
Wiltshire, United Kingdom

Probably one of the most famous sites in the world, Stonehenge, a ring of standing stones set within a ring, is probably a prehistoric burial ground. Archaeologists date it as anywhere between 3000 BC to 2000 BC, and remains found on the site contain human bones from as early as 3000 BC. The site and its surroundings are included in UNESCO's list of World Heritage Sites. A legally protected site, it is maintained by the Historic Buildings and Monuments Commission for England.

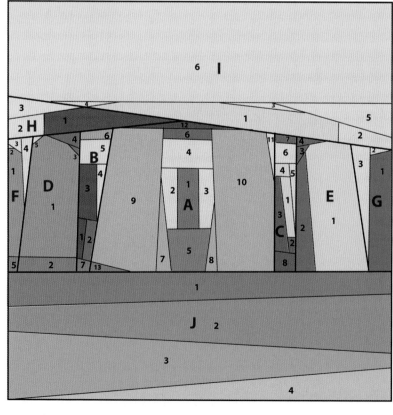

Eiffel Tower
Champ de Mars, Paris, France

The Eiffel Tower was erected in 1889 to serve as the entrance arch to the 1889 Exposition Universelle, which was a World's Fair celebrating the centennial of the French Revolution. Named for Gustave Eiffel, whose company designed and then built the Eiffel Tower, it was for 40 years the tallest structure in the world until the Chrysler Building was built in 1930. Although the original plan called for the tower to be torn down after 20 years, its popularity and its new use for communication purposes allowed it to stay. It remains today as one of the most recognizable and visited structures in the world.

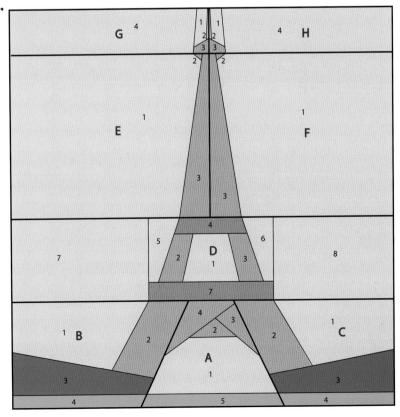

Basket Building
Newark, Ohio, USA

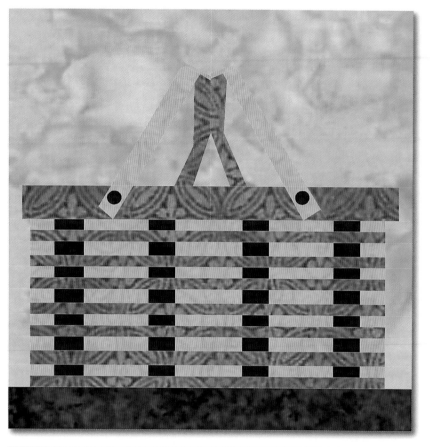

This building shaped like a basket is actually the corporate headquarters for the Longaberger Company. It was the brainchild of David Longaberger, the founder of the Longaberger Company, an American manufacturer and distributor of handcrafted maple wood baskets and other home and lifestyle products. The building, a seven-story stucco over steel structure, is a very enlarged replica—160 times larger—of one of the company's signature products, the "Medium Market Basket." The handles of the "basket" weigh almost 150 tons and can be heated during cold weather to prevent ice damage. Originally David Longaberger wanted all of the Longaberger buildings to be shaped like baskets but only the headquarters was completed at the time of his death in 1997. The Home Office, however, continues to attract the attention of media and tourists from around the world.

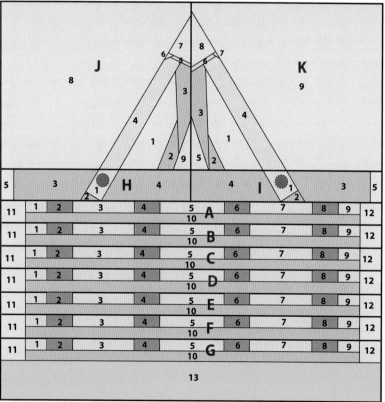

Hagia Sophia

Istanbul, Turkey

The church of Hagia Sophia ("Holy Wisdom") has served as a Greek Orthodox Church, an imperial mosque, a Roman Catholic cathedral and finally a museum. The current building was built between 532 and 537 on the orders of the Byzantine Emperor Justinian. It was actually the third church on that site; the first two, built in 360 and 415, were destroyed during riots. It is especially famous for its huge dome and is considered the capstone of Byzantine architecture. It remained an Eastern Orthodox Cathedral and the seat of the Patriarch of Constantinople until 1453. Between 1204 and 1261, however, it was converted to a Roman Catholic cathedral.

After Mehmed the Second's conquest of the city in 1453, it was converted to a mosque and remained that until 1931 when the Ottoman Empire fell. In 1935, the Turkish government converted the structure to a museum, and they restored the Christian mosaic icons, which had been covered with whitewash.

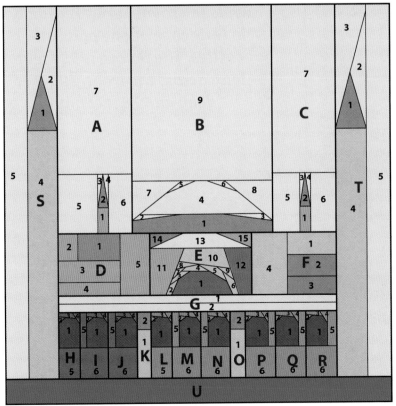

Buckingham Palace
London, England

Buckingham Palace is the official London residence of Britain's royal family as well as the administrative headquarters and workplace of the monarchy. Originally a townhouse built for the Duke of Buckingham in 1703 and eventually enlarged with three wings around a central courtyard, the building became the home of the British monarch in 1837 when Queen Victoria ascended the throne. Additions were made to the palace including the balcony on which the royal family greets crowds on important occasions. The palace, furnished with a magnificent art collection, is used today mainly for official and state entertaining while the royal family is usually in residence at one of its other castles. The palace is 354 feet long across the front, 393 feet deep and 78 feet high.

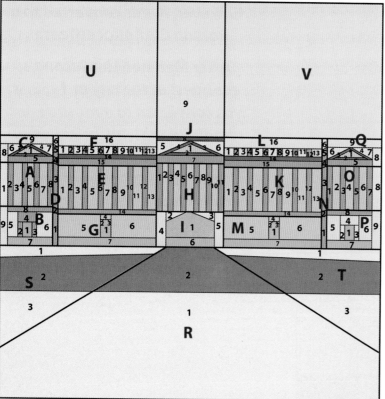

Fallingwater

Stewart Township, Pennsylvania, USA

Fallingwater was built as a mountain retreat for the Edgar J. Kaufmann family of Pittsburgh, owners of Kaufmann's Department Stores (now a part of Macy's). Their son Edgar Kaufman, Jr. had studied architecture and was a resident apprentice in architecture at Frank Lloyd Wright's Taliesin East School and Studio from 1933 to 1934. It was his suggestion that Frank Lloyd Wright be asked to design the house. The Kaufmanns had wanted a view of the falls on the property; instead Wright designed the house to sit on the falls because he wanted them to live with the falls, making it a part of their everyday life. Shortly after its completion, Time Magazine called it Wright's "most beautiful job." It was designated a National Historic Landmark in 1966, and in 1991, members of the American Institute of Architects named the house the "best all-time work of American architecture." Fallingwater was the family's weekend home from 1937 to 1963. In 1963, Kaufmann, Jr. donated the property to the Western Pennsylvania Conservancy. In 1964, it was opened to the public as a museum. Nearly five million people have visited the house. The Conservancy has preserved Fallingwater since 1963, with a major structural repair in 2002 strengthening Fallingwater's cantilevers to prevent collapse and future deflection.

Pantheon
Rome, Italy

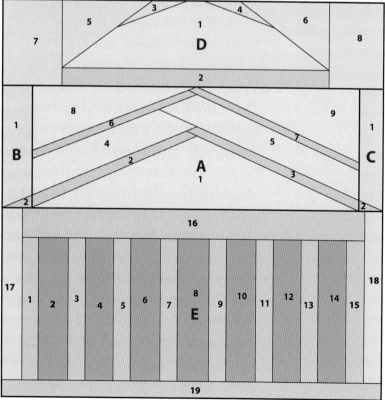

The Pantheon in Rome was commissioned by Marcus Agrippa during the reign of Augustus (27 BC to 14 AD) as a temple to all the gods of ancient Rome. It was rebuilt by the emperor Hadrian about 126 AD. In 609, the Byzantine emperor Phocas gave the building to Pope Boniface IV, who converted it into a Roman Catholic church and consecrated it to Santa Maria ad Martyres, now known as Santa Maria dei Martiri. It has been in continuous use throughout its history. Since the 7th century, the Pantheon has been used as a Roman Catholic church. The fact that the building was consecrated as a church actually saved it from the total destruction that befell the majority of ancient Rome's buildings during the early medieval period. As the best-preserved example of an Ancient Roman monumental building, the Pantheon has been enormously influential in Western architecture. The style of the Pantheon can be detected in many buildings of the 19th and 20th centuries; numerous government and public buildings, city halls, universities, and public libraries echo its portico-and-dome structure.

The Beehive Building
Wellington, New Zealand

This building is actually the executive wing of the New Zealand Parliament Building and houses the prime minister's offices as well as offices of cabinet ministers. The building is called the "beehive" because its shape is reminiscent of a traditional woven form of a basket used by beekeepers to house their hives. Designed by Scottish architect Sir Basil Spence, it is 10 stories high with four additional floors below ground. The roof is constructed from 20 tons of copper. Queen Elizabeth officially opened the building in 1977.

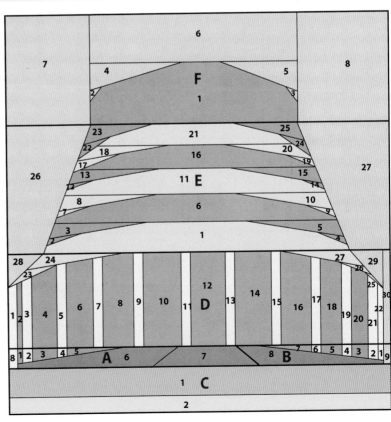

Mission San Luis Rey

Oceanside, California, USA

Mission San Luis Rey de Francia is a Spanish mission located in Oceanside, California, a city in San Diego county. One of 21 Spanish missions established in California, San Luis Rey was started on June 13, 1798 by Padre Fermin Lasuen.

The current church, completed in 1815, is the third church at this location. It functions as a parish church as well as a museum and a retreat center. It is a National Historic Landmark and is distinctive due to its combination of Spanish Renaissance, Moorish, Muslim and Spanish Colonial architecture. The church is the only surviving mission church laid out in the form of a cross. It is 165 feet in length with 27 feet in width and 30 feet high. Unique among Spanish missions is a cupola, a lantern made from 144 panes of glass, which tops the dome built over the sanctuary in 1829.

Note: *Embroider crosses at tops of domes. Appliqué circle above door.*

One World Trade Center

New York City, USA

The building is part of the effort to memorialize and rebuild following the destruction of the original World Trade Center complex in the attacks of September 11, 2001. This 104-story structure actually shares a name with the Twin Tower in the original World Trade Center destroyed in the September 11 terrorist attack.

On May 10, 2013 when the building's spire was completed and installed, the building became the highest in the United States and the fourth tallest skyscraper in the world. It now stands at 1,776 feet, a symbolic reference to 1776, the year of the United States Declaration of Independence.

Burj Khalifa
Dubai, United Arab Emirates

Known by the name Burj Dubai before its final construction, Burj Khalifa is the tallest man-made structure in the world. The building is intended to become the centerpiece of a large development in downtown Dubai, which would supposedly diversify the country from a strictly oil-based economy to one that might become more service and tourism based. Skidmore, Owings and Merrill of Chicago who also designed the Sears Tower (now the Willis Tower) and One World Trade Center handled the architecture and engineering on the project. The tower is 2,717 feet (828 meters) high and contains 163 floors.

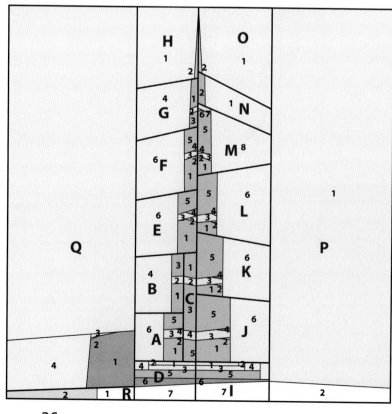

Big Ben

Westminster, London, United Kingdom

Big Ben is actually the nickname for the bell in the clock tower at Westminster Palace. For years the tower was simply known as the "Clock Tower." In 2012, it was officially renamed the Elizabeth Tower in honor of the queen on her diamond jubilee. The tower, which is the third tallest freestanding clock tower in the world, holds the largest chiming clock in the world. The bell was most probably named in honor of Sir Benjamin Hall, who as Commissioner of Works, oversaw the installation of the bell in the clock tower. The tower designed by Augustus Pugin is 315 feet high. The bottom 200 feet of the tower's structure consists of brickwork, and the four clock dials are 180 feet above ground. Two months after the clock was finally installed in the tower, it cracked. It was repaired, but Big Ben has chimed with a slightly different tone ever since and is still in use today complete with the crack.

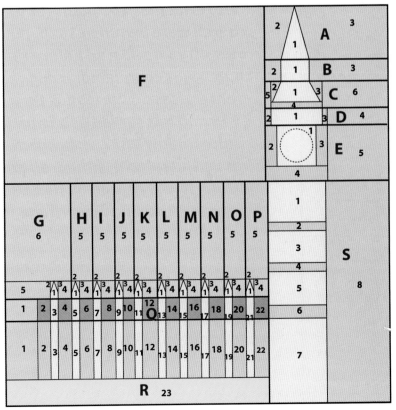

Note: *Appliqué circle for clock face.*

St. Thomas Cathedral
Mumbai (Bombay), India

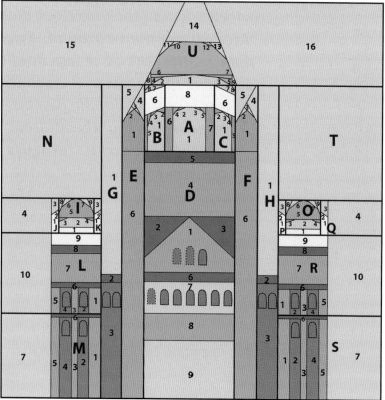

St. Thomas, the first Anglican Church in Mumbai (then called Bombay) was started to "improve the moral standards" of the growing Anglican community developed by the East India Company. To protect their property in Mumbai, a gate was built around their settlement. One of the gates, the entrance to St. Thomas, was called Churchgate. The street on which the church stands was, in fact, called Churchgate Street. That name remained for over 200 years until the street was renamed Veer Nariman Road. The whole area west of the church is today still called Churchgate by many of the long-time residents. The plans for the church were begun in 1676, but over 40 years passed before the church was completed. It opened for services on Christmas Day, 1718 and has served as a church since. In July 1837, the church was consecrated a cathedral, and in 2004 it was chosen by UNESCO for the Asia Pacific Heritage Conservation Award.

Note: Appliqué or embroider arched windows after block is completed.

The Capitol Building
Washington, DC, USA

The United States Capitol Building is one of the most impressive buildings in the nation and a magnificent example of 19th century neoclassical architecture. A five level building, the ground floor contains congressional offices. Both the House of Representatives and the Senate meet on the second floor; the House in the south wing and the Senate in the north wing. The Rotunda, a circular space that displays American art, is under the dome in the center of the building. The third floor provides a space where visitors can watch Congress when it is in session. Additional offices along with equipment for the building fill up the rest of the building. The Capitol covers a ground area of about 4 acres with a floor area of almost 17 acres.

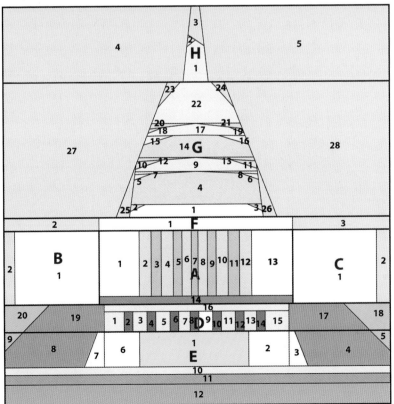

Great Pyramid of Giza
Giza, Egypt

The Great Pyramid of Giza (also known as the Pyramid of Khufu) is the oldest of the Seven Wonders of the Ancient World, and the only one to remain largely intact today. Most Egyptian pyramids were built as tombs for the rulers, Pharaohs, and their families. Historians feel that this tomb took 10 to 20 years to build, ending around 2560 BC. For over 3800 years, this Pyramid was the tallest man-made structure in the world. It is 756 feet long on each side, 450 feet high and is built of 2,300,000 blocks, each weighing about 2 ½ tons. No side is more than 8" different in length than any other side.

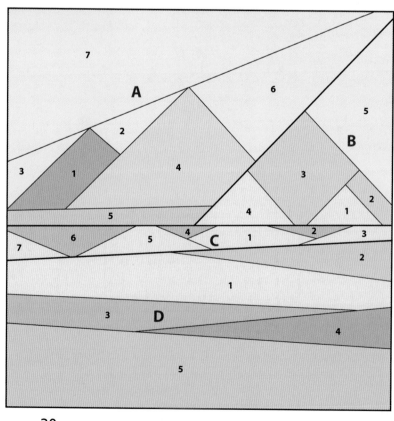

John Hancock Center
Chicago, Illinois, USA

When this building was completed in 1968 at 1,506 feet, it was actually the tallest building in the world outside of New York. Today it still remains among the top buildings, ranking fourth tallest in the city of Chicago and seventh tallest in the United States. The building contains offices, restaurants and over 600 apartments. The building is named for the John Hancock Mutual Life Insurance Company, who in addition to helping to finance the project, was an original tenant.

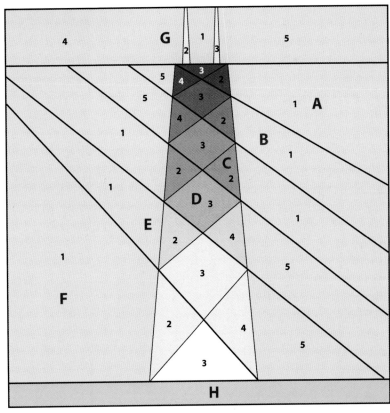

Jumeirah Beach Hotel

Dubai, United Arab Emirates

With its absolutely striking wave design, the Jumeirah Beach Hotel is one of Dubai's most instantly recognizable buildings. The hotel is situated less than ¼ mile off shore on an island owned at one time by the Chicago Bridge and Iron Company which for years had floating oil storage tankers on the site. When it was completed in 1997, the hotel was the 9th tallest building in Dubai.

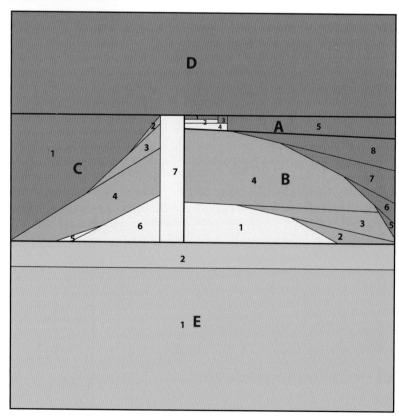

Oriental Pearl Tower

Shanghai, China

In addition to serving as a radio and TV tower servicing the Shanghai area with television and FM radio channels, the Oriental Pearl Tower is a unique bit of architecture attracting thousands of visitors each year. Eleven steel spheres hang through the center of the tower. There are three large spheres including the top sphere, five smaller spheres and three decorative spheres on the tower's base. A variety of features are contained in the spheres including a sightseeing hall, shops, restaurants and a hotel. The entire structure sits on a grassy base, looking like pearls shining on a jade plate. When the Tower was completed in 1994, it was—at 1,535 feet—the tallest structure in China, a designation it carried for 13 years.

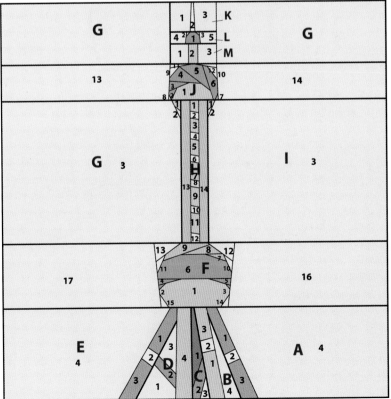

Great Sphinx of Giza
Al Ahram, Giza, Egypt

A Sphinx was thought by the Ancients to be a mythical creature with a lion's body and a human head, and the "Great Sphinx" is a limestone statue of a sphinx sitting on the Giza Plateau on the bank of the Nile River in Giza, Egypt. Historians now believe that the face of the Sphinx is supposed to represent the face of Pharaoh Khafra, who was the son of Pharaoh Khufu, and built during the reign of Khafra (about 2558 BC to 2532 BC). It is the largest monolith statue (carved from a singe massive stone or rock) in the world and the oldest. The Sphinx measures 241 feet long, 63 feet wide and 66 feet high.

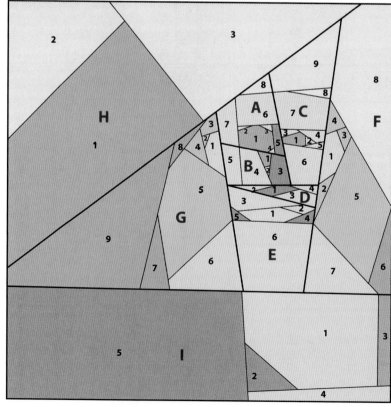

St. Peter's Basilica
Vatican City

One of the most famous examples of Renaissance architecture, St. Peter's Basilica is one of the largest churches in the world and is regarded as the greatest building of its age. Although it is neither the mother church nor the cathedral of the diocese of Rome, St. Peter's, located within Vatican City, remains one of the holiest of Catholic sites. Because of its location in the Vatican, it is the spot for many liturgical functions. The Pope presides over a number of occasions during the year whether in the Basilica or in St. Peter's Square. Construction of the current Basilica, replacing the 4th century structure, was begun in 1506 and completed in 1626. Among the artists who contributed to building the structure was most significantly Michelangelo.

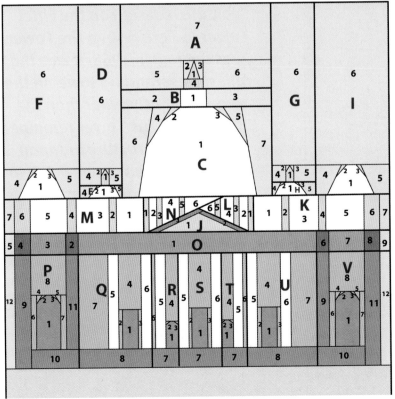

Tokyo Tower

Tokyo, Japan

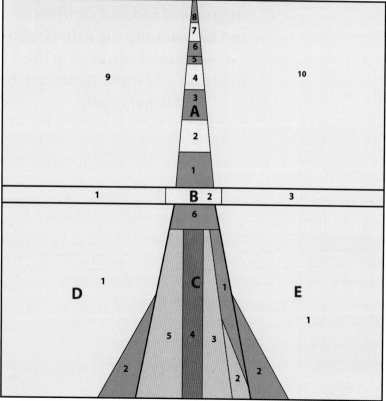

The Tokyo Tower is both an observation and communications tower as well as a tourist attraction in Tokyo, Japan. The communications boom in the 1950s led private broadcasting companies in Japan to begin operating their own TV towers. Fearful that transmission towers would soon be built all over Tokyo where they could overrun the city, the decision was reached to construct one large tower. The original plan was to build a tower taller than the Empire State Building, which was at the time, the tallest building in the world. Unfortunately lack of funds and materials changed the decision to base a design on the Eiffel Tower in Paris. When the Tower was opened in 1958, it was the tallest freestanding tower in the world, slightly taller than the Eiffel Tower. The Tower remained the tallest structure in Japan until 2010 when the new Tokyo Skytree Tower took over the title.

Topkapi Palace

Istanbul, Turkey

The Topkapi Palace was the major residence of the Ottoman Turkish Sultans for over 400 years of their reign from 1465 to 1856. The palace was begun under the rule of Sultan Mehmed II, the conqueror of Constantinople, in 1459 and expanded over the centuries. After the end of the Ottoman Empire in 1923, the government had the Palace changed into a museum under the rule of the Ministry of Culture and Tourism. While the palace has hundreds of rooms, the public is only allowed access to the most important ones. The palace contains a large collection of shields, armor, Islamic manuscripts and murals plus a display of Ottoman jewelry and other treasures.

Transamerica Pyramid

San Francisco, California, USA

The tallest skyscraper in San Francisco, the building was originally commissioned by the chief executives of the Transamerica Corporation as corporate headquarters. Although the building no longer houses the headquarters of the corporation, it is still associated with the company and appears as the company's logo. Completed in 1972, the building has become one of the symbols of the city. The building is a four-sided pyramid with two wings for the elevator shaft on the east and a stairwell and smoke tower on the west side. The building's top 212 feet form the spire.

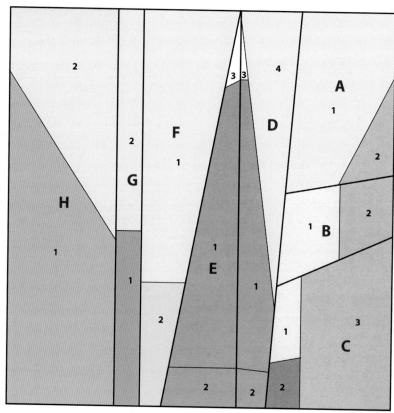

Washington Monument

Washington, DC, USA

The Washington Monument was built to honor George Washington, the first American president of the United States. It is a marble, granite and bluestone gneiss obelisk that is both the world's tallest stone structure and the world's tallest obelisk at 555 feet 5 1/8 inches tall. Although construction of the monument began in 1848, it was not completed until 1884; lack of funds and the civil war halted construction. It was officially opened on October 9, 1888, when it became the world's tallest structure. It held this title until 1889, when the Eiffel Tower was completed.

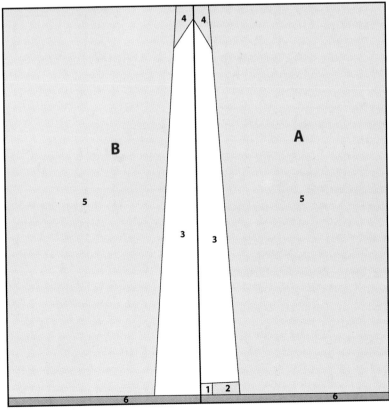

Woolworth Building

New York, New York, USA

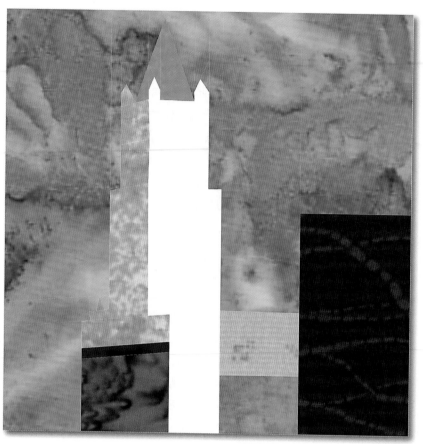

In 1913, Frank Woolworth, the founder of the F. W. Woolworth Company, a group of discount stores called "Five and Dimes" because most of the merchandise sold for five and ten cents, commissioned the famous architect Cass Gilbert to design a new corporate headquarters of 20 stories. The building was to be on his property on Broadway in Lower Manhattan opposite City Hall. More than a century later, the building stands at 792 feet with 60 stories and over 5,000 windows. It is one of the 50 tallest buildings in the United States and has been a National Historic Landmark since 1966 and is listed in the National Register of Historic Places.

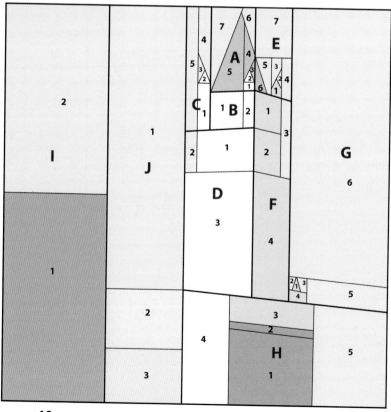

Solomon R. Guggenheim Museum
New York, New York, USA

The museum, often called simply the "Guggenheim" is a constantly expanding collection of impressionist, post impressionist, early modern and contemporary art. When it became apparent that a structure to house the collection would be needed, Frank Lloyd Wright was asked to design the building. It took Wright 15 years to create his plans for the museum, which finally opened in October 1959. The museum he designed is a cylindrical structure, wider at the top than at the bottom. It has a ramp gallery that starts just under the skylight in the ceiling and moves in a long spiral until it reaches ground. It is considered one of the most important architectural landmarks of today.

Hallgrimskirkja

Reykjavik, Iceland

Hallgrimskirkja, the largest church in Iceland, was designed to look like the Icelandic basalt lava flows. The church, named after the Icelandic poet, Hallgrimur Petursson, the author of the Passion Hymns, is one of the city's most famous landmarks, and can be seen throughout the city. The church, which can also be used as a viewing tower, has an observation deck which permits viewing Reykjavik and the surrounding mountains. Designed by State Architect Guojon Samuelsson, the church took 38 years to build. The landmark tower was actually completed long before the church. A statue of the explorer Leif Eriksson, which was a gift from the United States, sits in front of the church.

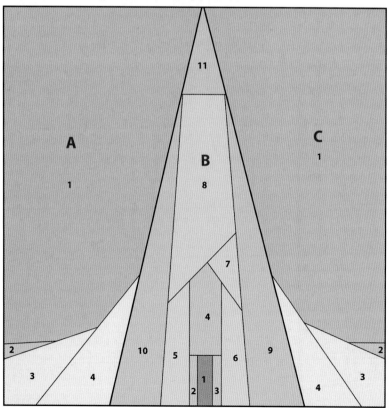

Burj Al Arab

Jumeira 3, Dubai, United Arab Emirates

Burj Al Arab, "The Tower of the Arabs," is a luxury hotel located on the same island as the Jumeirah Beach Hotel, described on page 32. The hotel was built to mimic the sail of a dhow, a sailing vessel used in the Red Sea and the Indian Ocean region.

The architect, Tom Wright, was asked to create a building that would become synonymous with the place as the Sydney Opera House is with Sydney and the Eiffel Tower is with Paris. Construction began in 1994 and was completed in December of 1999. It is 1,053 feet high and is the fourth tallest hotel in the world. Despite its size, there are only 202 bedroom suites in the hotel; the smallest suite is 1,820 square feet, while the largest covers 8,400 square feet.

Brandenburg Gate

Berlin, Germany

The Brandenburg Gate (Brandenburger Tor) was formerly a city gate, which was rebuilt in the 18th century as a triumphant arch. The gate was commissioned as a structure to represent peace and consists of twelve Doric columns. On top of the gate is the statue known as the Quadriga, a chariot drawn by four horses driven by the Roman goddess of Victory. During the post World War II partition of Germany, the gate was next to the Berlin Wall and became isolated and inaccessible. When the Wall fell in 1989, the gate represented freedom and the re-unification of the city of Berlin. In 2000, refurbishing of the Gate began with private funds, and on October 3, 2002, the Brandenburg Gate once again reopened, and is now one of the most famous landmarks in Germany.

Statue of Liberty

Liberty Island, Manhattan, New York, USA

The statue, a neoclassical sculpture that sits on Liberty Island in the midst of New York harbor, was a gift to the people of the United States from the people of France, celebrating the union's victory in the revolution and the abolition of slavery. The statue was designed by Frederic Bartholdi, at the bequest of the French law professor Edouard Rene de Laboulaye, who promoted the idea in 1865 that the French would produce the statue while the Americans provide the site. Work did not begin on the project until 1870, and the statue was not dedicated until October, 1886. Raising the money proved especially difficult; over 120,000 American contributors sent in donations, much of which were less than a dollar. The statue was built in France, crated and shipped overseas, where the Americans had engaged Gustave Eiffel, the man who designed the Eiffel Tower, to design the pedestal for the statue. A poem by the American poet Emma Lazurus is engraved on a bronze plaque inside the lower level.

Note: *Embroider points of crown after completing block.*

Sagrada Familia
Barcelona, Spain

The Basilica and Expiatory Church of the Holy Family is a large incomplete Roman Catholic Church in Barcelona, Spain. Although the church is not expected to be completed until 2026 to 2028, the church is a UNESCO World Heritage Site. In addition, Pope Benedict XVI consecrated it and declared it a minor basilica. The building of the church had begun in 1882, but the architect Antoni Gaudi took over the project in 1883. He transformed the structure combining Gothic and curvilinear art nouveau styles. Gaudi devoted over 40 years to the project, and when he died, less than a quarter of the project was completed.

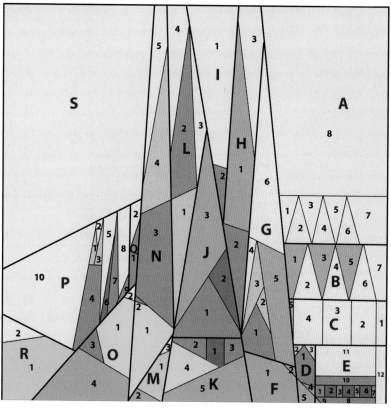

CN Tower

Toronto, Ontario, Canada

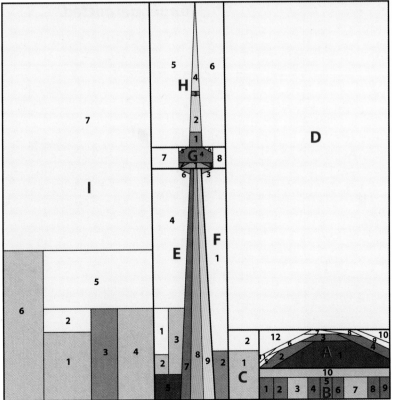

When the CN Tower, a concrete communications and observation tower, was completed in 1976, it was not only the world's tallest freestanding structure at 1,815 feet, but the world's tallest tower as well. Both of those records were held for 34 years until Burj Khalifa (page 26) was built. The idea for the creating of the CN Tower began in 1968 when the Canadian National Railway decided that they wanted to build a platform for TV and Radio to service the Canadian industry. The plan became official in 1972, and the tower was completed four years later. The name "CN" referred to Canadian National, who had built the tower. However, in 1995, the railway decided to divest itself of non-core freight railway assets. It therefore transferred the tower to the Canada Lands Company. The abbreviation, CN, was therefore expanded to represent the words, "Canadian National Tower" or Canada's National Tower." Neither of these names is widely used today.

In 1995, the tower was included in the list of the Seven Wonders of the World by the American Society of Civil Engineers.

El Castillo, Chichen Itza, Tinum

Yucatan, Mexico

The ruins of Chichen Itza, a large pre-Columbian Mayan city, is federal property maintained by Mexico's National Institute of Anthropology and History. Dominating the center of the Chichen Itza is El Castillo (Mexican for the castle), a Mesoamerican step-pyramid. The structure is over 78 feet high plus an additional 20 feet for the temple. The structure sits on a square base slightly over 181 feet across. It is made by a series of terraces with stairs up each of the four sides to the temple which sits at the top. El Castillo is one of the most visited pre-Columbian structures in Mexico even though climbing the monument is no longer permitted.

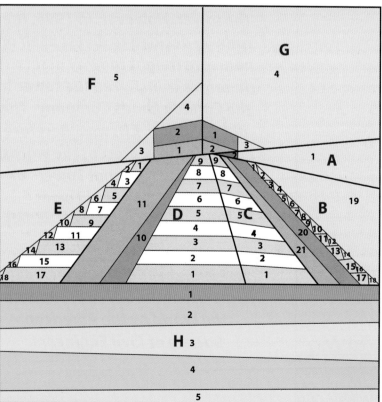

Cathedral de Brasilia

Brasília, Brazil

The "Metropolitan Cathedral of Our Lady Aparecida" is the Roman Catholic cathedral for Brasilia, and the seat of the Archdiocese of Brasilia. The cathedral designed by Oscar Niemeyer, is a hyperboloid structure constructed from 16 concrete columns weighing 90 tons each, which represent two hands moving upwards toward heaven. The structure has a glass roof which appears to be reaching up toward heaven. Most of the cathedral is below ground with the roof of the cathedral, the roof of the baptistery and the bell tower visible above ground. The cathedral was consecrated in October 1968, and was officially opened in May 1970. The cathedral was declared a National Historic and Artistic Monument in 1990. There are about 1,000,000 visitors to the cathedral every year.

Note: *Embroider cross at top center.*

Torii Gates
Miyajima Island, Japan

A Torii is a Japanese gate traditionally located at the entrance of (or even within) a Shinto shrine. There it indicates the transition from the profane to the sacred. They are also often located at the entrances to Buddhist temples. Traditionally, Torii were made from wood or stone, but today other materials including reinforced concrete, copper, stainless steel and other materials are used. Probably the most well known Torii gates are the ones sitting in front of Miyajima Island, which is a small island about an hour outside the city of Hiroshima. It is especially well known for its giant Torii gate, which at high tide gives the impression that it is floating on the water. The official name of the island is Itsukushima, but it is most often referred to as Miyajima, which is Japanese for "Shrine Island." The main buildings of the island's key shrine, like the Torii gate, are built over the water.

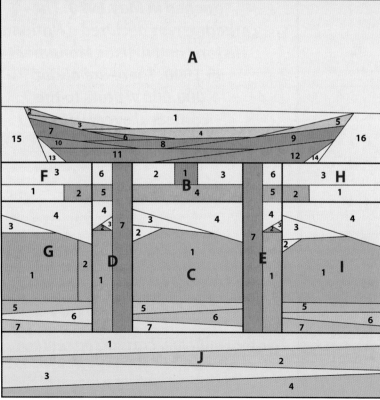

Macau Tower

Macau, People's Republic of China

Macau was a Portuguese colony until 1999 when it was returned to China. Today, the economy is greatly dependent on gambling and tourism. On a visit to New Zealand, the casino billionaire Stanley Ho Hung-Sun was impressed by the Sky Tower in Auckland, and arranged for a similar one to be built in Macau. The work began in 1998, and the tower was officially opened in 2001. Its official name is Macau Tower Convention and Entertainment Centre. It is 1,109 feet high and includes an observation deck, restaurants, theaters, and shopping malls. One of the main attractions is "Skywalk X," a walking tour around the outer rim. In addition, the tower is used for telecommunications and broadcasting. The tower is one of the members of the World Federation of Great Towers.

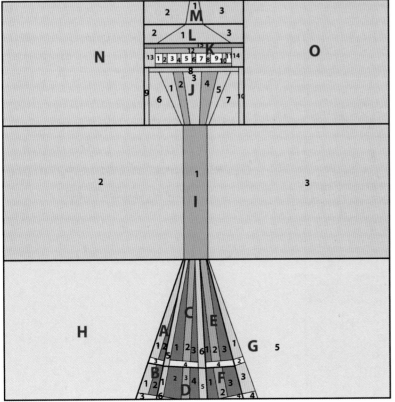

Hall of Supreme Harmony

Beijing, China

The Forbidden City, home to the Hall of Supreme Harmony, was the imperial palace of China for almost 500 years. Today, the site is most commonly known as "The Former Palace," and the Palace Museum is in charge of the site, working to restore and repair all of the buildings. The largest hall within the Forbidden City is the Hall of Supreme Harmony, one of the largest wooden structures within China. Since the hall was the symbol of power, no other building in the entire empire could be any higher. The hall is 115 feet high (123 feet including the rooftop decoration). It is 210 feet wide and 122 feet long. There are 72 pillars in rows of six supporting the roof. It is built above a marble stone base and surrounded by bronze incense burners. The Forbidden City was declared a World Heritage Site by UNESCO in 1987 because of its important place in the development of Chinese culture and architecture.

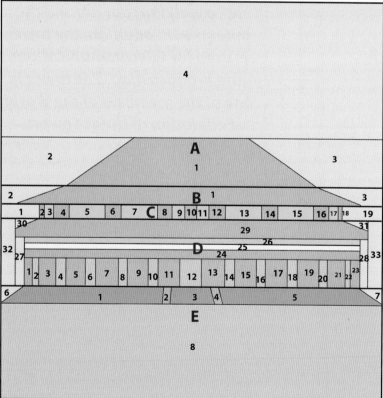

30 St. Mary Axe

London, England

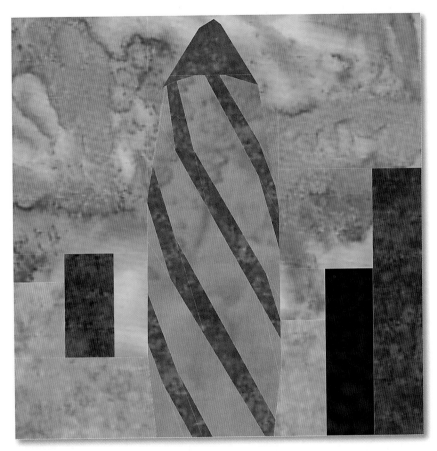

30 St. Mary Axe is a 591 foot tall skyscraper that sits on St. Mary Axe Street in London's main financial district. The building is on the former site of the Baltic Exchange, which was the headquarters for world shipping interests and information. In 1992, a bomb, placed close to the Exchange by the Provisional IRA caused extensive damage to the building. Rather than attempt to restore the old building, plans were developed to create a new building with a tower which would maintain London's traditional look with its narrow streets. The building uses energy-saving methods that allow it to use only half the power that a traditional tower might use. Even though the building seems to have a curved glass shape, there is only one piece of curved glass in the building: the lens-shaped cap at the top.

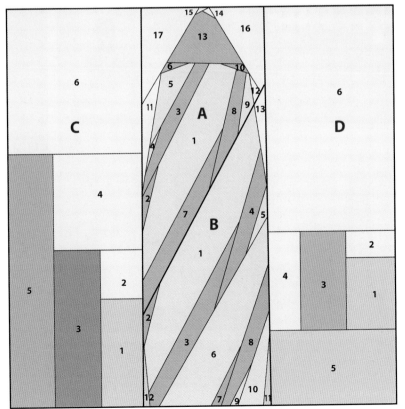

USA Treasures

Approximate Size:

34 1/2" x 44 1/2"

Blocks:

Capitol Building (page 29)
Hotel Del Coronado (page 13)
Guggenheim Museum (page 41)
Mission San Luis Rey (page 24)
Statue of Liberty (page 45)
Space Needle (page 12)
Basket Building (page 18)
White House (page 5)
Sears Tower (page 14)
John Hancock Center (page 31)
Empire State Building (page 8)
Washington Monument (page 39)

Block Size:

8" x 8"

MATERIALS:

Blocks

assorted scraps and fat quarters: white, lt blue, med blue, red, lt green, med green, dk green, tan, lt brown, med brown, dk brown, lt gray, med gray, dk gray, black

Finishing

5/8 yard red
1/4 yard lt blue
5/8 yard dk blue
1/2 yard dk red
1 1/2 yard backing
batting

CUTTING:

Note: *You do not need to cut exact pieces for foundation piecing.*

Finishing

8 strips. 1 1/2" x 8 1/2", red (sashing)
3 strips, 1 1/2" x 26 1/2", red (sashing)
2 strips, 1 1/2" x 35 1/2", red (1st border)
2 strips, 1 1/2" x 28 1/2", red (1st border)
4 strips, 1"-wide, lt blue (2nd border)
5 strips, 3 1/2"-wide, dk blue (3rd border)
5 strips, 2 1/2"-wide. dk red (binding)

INSTRUCTIONS:

1. Make 12 blocks referring to Foundation Piecing and using the 8" foundation patterns on the CD.

2. Referring to photo, sew blocks together with 1 1/2" x 8 1/2" red sashing strips in between.

3. Sew the rows of blocks together with 1 1/2" x 26 1/2" red strips in between.

4. Sew the 1"-wide lt blue border strips to the sides and then to the top and bottom of the quilt.

5. Sew the 3 1/2"-wide dk blue border to quilt top sides first, then top and bottom.

6. Finish quilt referring to Finishing your Quilt on the CD.

European Adventures

Approximate Size:
39 ½" x 49 ½"

Blocks:
St. Paul's Cathedral (page 4)
Eiffel Tower (page 17)
Stonehenge (page 16)
Notre Dame Cathedral (page 15)
Leaning Tower of Pisa (page 6)
Colosseum (page 9)
Pantheon (page 22)
Buckingham Palace (page 20)
Brandenburg Gate (page 44)
St. Peter's Basilica (page 35)
Big Ben (page 27)
St. Mary Axe (page 53)

Block Size:
8" x 8"

MATERIALS:
Blocks

assorted scraps and fat quarters:
white, lt blue, med blue, red, lt green,
med green, dk green, tan, lt brown,
med brown, dk brown, lt gray, med
gray, dk gray, black

Finishing

⅝ yard gold
1 yard black
1 ½ yards dk green
1 ½ yards backing
batting

CUTTING:
Note: *You do not need to cut exact pieces for foundation piecing.*

Finishing

12 strips, 1" x 8 ½", gold (frame)
12 strips, 1" x 9 ½", gold (frame)
12 strips, 1" x 8 ½", black (frame)
12 strips, 1" x 9 ½", black (frame)
8 strips, 1 ½" x 9½", dk green (sashing)
3 strips, 1 ½" x 29 ½", dk green (sashing)
2 strips, 1 ½" x 39 ½", dk green (1st border)
2 strips, 1 ½" x 31 ½", dk green (1st border)
5 strips, 1 ½"-wide, gold (2nd border)
6 strips, 3 ½"-wide, black (3rd border)
6 strips, 2 ½"-wide, dk green (binding)

INSTRUCTIONS:
1. Make 12 blocks referring to Foundation Piecing and using the 8" foundation patterns on the CD.

2. Sew 1" x 8 ½" gold strips to sides of six blocks; sew 1" x 9 ½" gold strips to top and bottom. Repeat for remaining six blocks using black strips.

3. Referring to photo, sew blocks together with 1 ½" x 9 ½" dk green sashing strips in between.

4. Sew the rows of blocks together with 1 ½" x 29 ½" dk green strips in between.

5. Sew the 1"-wide lt blue border strips to the sides and then to the top and bottom of the quilt.

6. Sew the dk blue border to quilt top sides first, then top and bottom.

7. Finish quilt referring to Finishing your Quilt on the CD.

Sky High Buildings

Approximate Size:
40 $\frac{1}{2}$" x 40 $\frac{1}{2}$"

Blocks:
Empire State Building (page 8)

Space Needle (page 12)

Sears Tower (page 14)

Oriental Pearl Tower (page 33)

Burj Al Arab (page 43)

John Hancock Center (page 31)

Tokyo Tower (page 36)

One World Trade Center (page 25)

Burj Khalifa (page 26)

Block Size:
8" x 8"

MATERIALS:
Blocks
assorted scraps and fat quarters: white, lt blue, med blue, red, lt green, med green, dk green, tan, lt brown, med brown, dk brown, lt gray, med gray, dk gray, black

Finishing
$\frac{5}{8}$ yard tan

$\frac{1}{4}$ yard dk blue

1 yard med blue

1 yard backing

batting

CUTTING:
Note: *You do not need to cut exact pieces for foundation piecing.*

Finishing
24 strips, 2 $\frac{1}{2}$" x 8 $\frac{1}{2}$", tan (sashing)

16 squares, 2 $\frac{1}{2}$" x 2 $\frac{1}{2}$", dk blue (cornerstones)

4 strips, 4 $\frac{1}{2}$"-wide, med blue (border)

5 strips, 2 $\frac{1}{2}$"-wide, med blue (binding)

INSTRUCTIONS:
1. Make 9 blocks referring to Foundation Piecing and using the 8" foundation patterns on the CD.

2. Referring to photo, place blocks in three rows of three blocks with 2 $\frac{1}{2}$" x 8 $\frac{1}{2}$" tan strips in between and 2 $\frac{1}{2}$" x 2 $\frac{1}{2}$" dk blue cornerstones at corners.

3. Sew blocks and sashing rows together; sew sashing and cornerstone rows.

4. Sew the rows of blocks together with rows of sashing in between.

5. Sew the 4 $\frac{1}{2}$"-wide med blue border strips to the sides and then to the top and bottom of the quilt.

6. Finish quilt referring to Finishing your Quilt on the CD.

Sacred Places

Approximate Size:
59 1/2" x 47 1/2"

Blocks:
Notre-Dame Cathedral (page 15)
St. Paul's Cathedral (page 4)
St. Basil's Cathedral (page 7)
St. Thomas Cathedral (page 28)
Sagrada Familia (page 46)
Cathedral de Brasilia (page 49)
Hall of Supreme Harmony (page 52)
St. Peter's Basilica (page 35)
Hagia Sophia (page 19)
Hallgrimskirkja (page 42)
Mission San Luis Rey (page 24)
Pantheon (page 22)

Block Size:
10" x 10"

MATERIALS:
Blocks
assorted scraps and fat quarters: white, lt blue, med blue, red, lt green, med green, dk green, tan, lt brown, med brown, dk brown, lt gray, med gray, dk gray, black

Finishing
1 1/2 yards red
1/4 yard lt gold
1 1/2 yards green
2 1/2 yards backing
batting

CUTTING:
Note: *You do not need to cut exact pieces for foundation piecing.*

Finishing
9 strips, 3" x 10 1/2", red (sashing)
*2 strips, 3" x 47 1/2", red (sashing)
2 strips, 3" x 35 1/2", red (1st border)
*2 strips, 3" x 53", red (1st border)
5 strips, 1"-wide lt gold (2nd border)
6 strips, 3"-wide, green (3rd border)
6 strips, 2 1/2"-wide, green (binding)
*Piece strips to achieve length needed.

INSTRUCTIONS:
1. Make 12 blocks referring to Foundation Piecing and using 10" foundation patterns. Print out the 5" block, enlarge it 200% and print on 11" x 17" paper at your local copy store.

2. Referring to photo, sew blocks together with 3" x 10 1/2" red sashing strips in between.

3. Sew the rows of blocks together with 3" x 47 1/2" red sashing strips in between.

4. Sew 3"-wide red border to quilt sides first, then top and bottom.

5. Sew the 1"-wide lt gold border strips to the sides and then to the top and bottom of the quilt.

6. Sew the 3"-wide green border to quilt top sides first, then top and bottom.

7. Finish quilt referring to Finishing your Quilt on the CD.

Ancient Wonders

MATERIALS:

Blocks

assorted scraps and fat quarters: white, lt blue, lt green, med green, dk green, tan, lt brown, med brown, dk brown, lt gray, med gray

Finishing

$1/4$ yard med brown

$1/4$ yard golden brown

$3/8$ yard blue

$3/4$ yard olive green

1 $1/4$ yard backing

batting

CUTTING:

Note: *You do not need to cut exact pieces for foundation piecing.*

Finishing

9 strips, 2 $1/2$" x 6 $1/2$", med brown (sashing)

4 strips, 2 $1/2$" x 18 $1/2$", golden brown (sashing)

4 strips, 2 $1/2$"-wide, blue (1st border)

4 strips, 3 $1/2$"-wide, olive green (2nd border)

4 strips, 2 $1/2$"-wide, olive green (binding)

Approximate Size:

28 $1/2$" x 36 $1/2$"

Blocks:

Great Pyramid of Giza (page 30)

Pantheon (page 22)

Stonehenge (page 16)

El Castillo, Chichen Itza (page 48)

Great Sphinx of Giza (page 34)

Colosseum (page 9)

Block Size:

6" x 6"

INSTRUCTIONS:

1. Make 6 blocks referring to Foundation Piecing and using the 6" foundation patterns on the CD.

2. Referring to photo, sew blocks together with 2 $1/2$" x 6 $1/2$" med brown sashing strips in between. Sew the rows of blocks together with 2 $1/2$" x 18 $1/2$" golden brown strips in between.

3. Sew the 2 $1/2$"-wide blue border strips to the sides and then to the top and bottom of the quilt. Repeat for olive green border.

4. Finish quilt referring to Finishing your Quilt on the CD.

Places I've Seen

Approximate Size:
26 1/2" x 55 1/2"

Blocks:
Washington Monument (page 39)
White House (page 5)
Transamerica Pyramid (page 38)
Statue of Liberty (page 45)
Mission San Luis Rey (page 24)
Sears Tower (page 14)
Empire State Building (page 8)
Hotel Del Coronado (page 13)
Capitol Building (page 29)
John Hancock Center (page 31)

Block Size: 8" x 8"

CUTTING:
Note: *You do not need to cut exact pieces for foundation piecing.*

Finishing
5 strips, 1 1/2" x 8 1/2", dk blue (sashing)
4 strips, 1 1/2" x 18", dk blue (sashing)
5 strips, 1 1/2"-wide, dk blue (1st border)
5 strips, 3 1/2"-wide, med green (2nd border)
4 strips, 2 1/2"-wide, med green (binding

INSTRUCTIONS:
1. Make 10 blocks referring to Foundation Piecing and using the 8" foundation patterns on the CD.

2. Referring to photo, sew blocks together with 1 1/2" x 8 1/2" dk blue sashing strips in between. Sew the rows of blocks together with 1 1/2" x 18" dk blue strips in between.

3. Sew the 1 1/2"-wide dk blue border strips to the sides and then to the top and bottom of the quilt. Repeat for med green border.

4. Finish quilt referring to Finishing your Quilt on the CD.

MATERIALS:

Blocks
assorted scraps and fat quarters: white, lt blue, med blue, lt green, med green, dk green, tan, lt brown, med brown, dk brown, lt gray, med gray, dk gray, black, red

Finishing
3/8 yard dk blue
1 yard med green
1 1/2 yard backing
batting

Index

About the CD

To run this application on Windows:

This is a self-loading CD. Simply place the CD into the CD-ROM drive. If the Auto-Run feature is not active on your system, follow these instructions to install:

- Click the Start button.
- Select Run from the menu.
- When the Run window opens, click Browse.
- Select your CD-ROM drive and then select 50 Big City Blocks..
- Click OK and follow the onscreen instructions.
- Decide which Blocks you are making and choose the template patterns that you need to complete it; double click to open.
- If the block does not open, you may need to instal Acrobat Reader. Download it easily from the internet using the website: http://www.adobe.com/products/acrobat/readstep2.html
- Print the template patterns you will need for your project.

To run this application on Mac OS 9 and OS X:

- Insert the CD into the CD-ROM drive. Double click on the *50 Big City Blocks* icon when it appears on the desktop.
- Choose the folder name that corresponds to the section that your block is in and click to open.
- Look for the Template folder and choose the templates that you need to make your blocks.
- If the block does not open, you may need to instal Acrobat Reader. Download it easily from the internet using the website: http://www.adobe.com/products/acrobat/readstep2.html
- Print the number of blocks and patterns you will need for your project.

For additional information and instructions, please read Frequently Asked Questions (FAQ.pdf) on the CD.